Rise to the top!

Joe Meier

Rise to the top!
Simple rules to succeed in any organization.

Copyright 2012 Joerg Meier

Second edition - August 2012

ISBN-13 9781479130641

Edited by Karla Meier

To my wonderful wife Karla - you are the best decision I ever made and the love of my life - and to my precious children Leah, Luke and Liam - you make me smile every day.

3

Rise to the top

Why do we go to work every day? I don't know about you, but I want to positively affect people's lives beginning with my own. I want to do something worth doing, chart my own course, and not be dependent on something or someone else for every step.

I don't want to work every day of my life.

I want to get paid for what I like to do!

Maybe you have read the 4-Hour Workweek by Timothy Ferriss, I don't want a 4-Hour Workweek, I want to be able to enjoy what I am doing 24-Hours a Day. How can I achieve this? By doing something that I enjoy, and getting paid to do it. Of course you won't see many job postings describing work like this, but you can make your job become this and it starts with being successful in what you are doing.

If you are successful, you will achieve freedom in what you are doing, you will get promoted; you will earn enough money to achieve financial freedom (not necessarily becoming a millionaire but being able to live without binding financial restrictions). You will gain responsibility and accountability for your actions and thus the opportunity to really change the world one small piece at a time.

As you might imagine I have read the 4-Hour Workweek (it is just a very good title for a book) and many other Business books that supposedly help you to either become CEO of a major company or build your own successful business. Realizing that most of the books I read were national or even international bestsellers I figured that something must be wrong with them. Millions have read these books, however they did not all turn into successful Business Entrepreneurs or business icons.

With that realization in mind I thought about my own career. What did I do to get where I am? (I am not a CEO of a Fortune 500 company – I guess you have figured as much already). Why do I think I should write a book about it (and why should you read it)?

I am what most of us would call the typical "Middle Manager" – not in a company Leadership role (yet) but on a fairly high level in the Management hierarchy. And by getting here I have achieved all the things I have already mentioned above – I am free in what I am doing, I am measured based on my success not on the way I get my job done, I hold responsibility and accountability for my own actions, and I have certainly achieved financial freedom.

I believe that by writing down my personal tips for success I can help you become more successful in your current position, prepare yourself for the next step in your career and get you there fast.

I have used most of these principles for almost twenty years and they have helped me reach many career milestones I wouldn't have thought possible when I embarked on my Management career.

You know as well as I do that there are many good books on management that analyze management theory, time management, how to lead and change an organization, and "How to become CEO by the end of the year". Many of these I would recommend if you want to explore a certain topic in more depth.

However – I want something easier, and more practical; simple guidelines that you can apply immediately to build your career.

Management and Leadership is not rocket science. Just learn and apply what fits you and your management style from this book. There is no unproven theory in here – everything I have written I have applied in my own career.

Many of these easy and simple rules might contradict what you have read and learned elsewhere. You have to choose for yourself which way is right for you. Some of these rules will not make you very popular – but then again you want to build a career and not win a beauty pageant.

So test what works for you as you apply it to your personal style of leadership. I believe they will help you succeed in any organization.

Why should you listen to me?

Now, why should you even listen to my advice? For starters these are time proven simple and pragmatic rules – nothing fancy. I have shared these principles in part with many of my colleagues over the years and I have tried to only put in here what really works. Tips that will make you a great manager on any hierarchical level in your organization.

I have not always been a manager. Like many of you I started in a fairly technical job over twenty years ago (in Information technology).I had the great opportunity to experience the dawn of the Information age from the very beginning. Early on, I realized working with the newest technology in IT would be a fun career opportunity for me personally. At first I held various technical positions but soon moved up to be a Team leader, Department Leader, IT Director and various other management positions.

I have worked in many different fields of IT: corporate IT departments, major IT Services companies (Compaq and HP), as both a consultant and project manager. Currently I am working as Chief Technology Officer at an IT service company in Germany.

My career path was not clear from the beginning. At first I was mostly focused on the technology aspect of my job, finding it very satisfying. However, soon I realized that real freedom at work surprisingly comes only with **added** responsibility. Eventually I decided to focus more on my Management career.

Instead of getting a formal four year university degree after High School I did military service and then attended an IT technical school. Because of this, at the beginning, I only had technical knowledge and skills to offer. As these were the early 90's and computer technology was still fairly new, this wasn't really an issue. With most careers, you can make it to the first or second level of management in any company just based on a solid technical background.

As time passed I noticed that I had to do something to be able to understand my business counterparts better and engage in topics that are more related to the Business world, rather than just the Information Technology world. My main motivation was to differentiate between real business issues from stuff made up by other managers, who were already in over their heads. I recognized they tried to hide behind buzzwords and explanations of complexities that only existed in their minds. So I went on to study for my Masters in Business Administration (at Heriott-Whatt University, Edinburgh, Scotland) during nights and weekends which equipped me with a new found business knowledge. When I was promoted to the next level, it was clear to me that even inside a big corporation I wanted to be responsible for my actions and results as much as possible. Managing a larger group of employees became a necessity for me to be able to do what I like most.

I have always loved my job – I have worked for many different companies in more than thirty countries. During my time as Project Manager and Consultant, I have seen quite a few more. Of course I have at times become frustrated, stressed out or just plain "lost it".

However, that didn't change my approach to work. This lead to an exciting and fulfilled career.

I am no Steve Jobs or Jack Welch – I am sure you have read their books and many of you might even be fully able to copy their success. I however am happy with my "human" achievements and I appreciate this opportunity to share with you some of the principles that have made me a successful manager.

I have also periodically added a *"from Joe's world"* section to some of the chapters to give you real life examples from my own career. Hopefully this will help make the discussed ideas and principles clearer and easier to implement.

Be efficient

"Efficiency is doing things right; effectiveness is doing the right things."

Peter F. Drucker

The first step in your rise to becoming a top performer and manager is quite simple – be efficient!

If you want to be better in what you are doing than everyone else you work with (and only then will you get noticed and get ahead) you have to make sure you are more efficient than everybody else.

Only if you are highly efficient, are you able to divert time to building your career, understand your organization, learn new things and be available to go the extra mile when needed.

Only when you are efficient in your current job, will you be able to take on the next job.

Here are a few rules that will help you be more efficient than many of your colleagues allowing you to think about how else you can benefit your company or to do that extra project that gives yourself added visibility in the organization and towards management.

Do the most annoying thing first

This is the simplest rule of them all. It is the most important one and the one that will aid you the most in getting things done. If you do follow this rule, you will become highly efficient every single day, staying on top of it all. In my opinion this is the best self-motivation possible.

But – because it is the most annoying task - most managers avoid ever doing it!

Change that habit! Make it your rule to do the most annoying thing first thing in the morning when you start your workday.

Start the task before getting your first coffee, talking to your team or doing anything else. Think for a few minutes what the most annoying task is that needs to get done that day, week or month and do it right away. It doesn't matter if it takes 5 minutes or half of your day – just make sure that this one thing is what you do first and finish first before you do anything else.

Even if this is the only thing you take away from this book, you will see that your productivity will increase immediately. You feel more motivated and productive and will start every day with the right attitude.

(If you want to go into more detail on how to find the most annoying task read "Eat that frog!" by Brian Tracy.)

I usually identify that thing by putting together my list for the day (see also "Always work from a list").

Looking at all the items that need to be done today helps you to focus and more easily identify the most annoying task.

Don't procrastinate!

Don't try to do some other easy things first!

You have to focus on this one thing otherwise you will get sidetracked and before you can get anything done you are caught up with all the other easier tasks that needed to be done.

Beware people will interfere with what you are doing, disasters will need to be averted, someone will need your help. In general many other distractions will come your way, try to not let that happen.

Make sure you set as top priority that one annoying task! This will get you motivated for the day. If you don't knock it off your list, I guarantee other annoying tasks will pile up in your to-do list which will eventually demotivate you every time you look at that list. This will reduce your efficiency dramatically.

Do the most annoying thing first - every day!

From Joe's world:

I tend to procrastinate tasks that I do not like. For me, this is more or less anything that is connected to "formalities". Unfortunately the more successful you become as a manager the more "formalities" come with the job. This includes signing expense reports, creating budget forecasts or writing investment requests.

In my current position I have to create investment requests usually in January for all investment projects of the coming year. Even though I know this (after all it happens every year) I used to procrastinate and thereby hurt running projects (without investment request there is no money for the project's investments).

A few years back I finally put it as a recurring task on my to-do list, and when the time came I tackled it as "the most annoying thing" (which it is) and got done with it quickly. I have been doing it the same way ever since – first working day after the projects for the coming years are settled this item is on my list and gets done.

Do that other thing

So you have finished that most annoying thing. Good for you! Now do that other thing.

What is the other thing?

Very simple, this is the one other task on your task list (see also: "Always work from a list") that if done immediately helps your manager the most.

Not yourself – at least not directly - but your manager!

It is important to identify this task as it helps you to achieve many things:

1.   Your manager will see you as someone who prioritizes correctly (at least from his point of view).

2.   Your manager sees you as someone who supports him in getting projects done quickly and efficiently. He will recognize that you can perform without much supervision, constant reminding or those awkward moments of: "Did you ever get around to …"

3.   You will also establish yourself as your manager's "Go-to guy". This is important as you will over time receive the most important projects from him or her as their goal is to get things done (Remember your managers' are also just looking to be efficient).

4.   You gain trust from your manager, which will be beneficial to you many times not only in your direct

relationship with each other, but also when he or she or yourself move on to other things.

So now you have finished your most annoying task (that feels good, doesn't it?) and you have completed the most important task for your manager (so he also feels good as he has gotten important work done as well).

This is the best start of any work day, everything else will be easy (and on top of that you just motivated yourself!).

You don't need more time – you just need to decide!

"You don't need more time, you just need to decide!"
(Seth Godin)

You always have to remember, you are a manager!

You are the one who gets paid to lead your team and make decisions! Even if you "manage" only one – yourself! The only reason we have Leaders in organizations is because we need someone to make decisions.

Decisions have to be made, and to make them you do not need more time.

Just decide!

Trust your gut feeling, trust your facts, trust your people - but never wait.

Every decision postponed poisons your organization. Projects will lose momentum; critical situations get out of control, people get frustrated and in the worst scenario: someone else will make the decision for you.

You will never have all the data needed to be completely sure that your decision will be right. Decisions are about what happens in the future and you will never be able to know the future. You know the statistics from the past, facts that held true in the past. But, face it; you have nothing that will ensure that your decision will be the right one.

But don't hesitate, hoping for a clear signal. You are wasting time and possibly foregoing wonderful business opportunities in the process.

Even more importantly, putting decision making off undermines your position as a leader. People who looked up to you, who followed you because of what you represented, will begin to question your leadership ability.

We need leaders. We do not want to make all the hard decisions ourselves – this is true in our personal lives as well as our work lives.

Make sure you are that leader and don't volunteer to give up your authority by being indecisive.

When it comes to making the call consider Lovaglia's Law:

"The more important the outcome of a decision, the more people will resist using evidence to make it."
(Michael Lovaglia is a professor at the University of Iowa)

So make sure that you keep focused on the decision, base it on the facts you have, the people you trust and – in the end – your gut-feeling – and then go through with it.

From Joe's world:

Once I was involved in a rather unfortunate project to reduce cost by eliminating a complete division of my company.

The goal was clear from the beginning; the only way to cut cost was to let people go. However, it took another six months from the initial realization to the final decision.

The only reason for this was that everyone involved, including myself, did not want to have to tell the people whose jobs we were eliminating, that they would have to go. We didn't want to fire anyone. So instead of making a clear decision and standing by it, we hesitated, hoping circumstances would change. In the end we were questioned why it took us so long, even though everyone already knew what had to happen.

As a manager, I was confronted with blame from the people I tried to protect – "Why didn't you tell us earlier?" – And from my superiors – "How did we get behind schedule with our cost saving efforts?"

All in all, at that time I didn't fulfill my role as a manager – I didn't decide.

Failure

Making many decisions in your role as a Leader will inevitably lead to making some wrong decisions.

Don't be afraid of failure, of making the wrong decision. Failure in a business environment is widely regarded as part of being a Leader as long as you stand by your decision and learn from the mistake.

Whatever you do, don't try to hide your failure, or try to blame someone else for your decision.

Accept failure, try to understand how your decision led to it and make sure next time you consider the reasons for your earlier failure when making a decision. Just don't postpone your next decision because you failed last time.

Simplify!

"Perfection is achieved, not when there is nothing left to add, but when there is nothing left to take away. "

(Antoine de St. Exupery)

"Make everything as simple as possible, but not simpler."

(Albert Einstein)

As my main field is Information Technology, I have seen many companies design complex to support elaborate business processes. Unfortunately, I have also seen many of these systems fail.

We sometimes forget that added complexity almost never translates into added benefits or success. Every time we make a process or product more complex we set ourselves up for failure.

Process and Product simplification should be one of the main goals of every professional and manager.

Do not reward complexity! Reward simplicity!

Ensure that everyone around you understands that you foster simple solutions. Depending on your organization this might require a new culture of work or just a small change.

In some organizations, it is considered an achievement to build such a complicated process that its creator becomes indispensable (for this also see: "The graveyard is full of indispensable people."). So much so, that he or she can't even go on vacation or worse, they are not available to take over other tasks or projects.

Make sure that you reward the opposite – a good manager is a dispensable manager. Only then can he take over new tasks and add value to the company.

In product design there are many examples of the success of simplicity. Just look Google or Apple and you will immediately recognize that one of their underlying design principles is simplicity.

So make sure that whenever and wherever possible you simplify!

Only promise what you can deliver!

Delivering on your promises is doing what you said you would do, when you said you would do it.

If you always do exactly what you say you will do you will build a very strong relationship with your colleagues, managers and customers. If you can deliver more than that, then better still!

Under promise and over deliver whenever possible!

Many companies use this principle to build trust and strong relationships between all levels of the organization and its customer and shareholder base. A classic business example is Apple's constantly low guidance for revenue and profit and over delivery every single quarter.

Be always true to your word – if you promise something, deliver it. Don't question your own promise after you have made it – you are obligated to fulfill it.

If you promised to deliver a sales presentation, make sure you are there on time and well prepared. If you promised to organize a meeting make sure you thought of everything needed. If you promised to sit in for your manager, make sure you are there and very well prepared.

Remember that a promise should be voluntarily – this is the second part of you promising something – only promise what you can deliver.

Do not let anyone pressure you into promising something you already know you will not be able to deliver. If you are sure you cannot do it – do not promise it. Say no (read also: "Never say No!"), make clear it is unreasonable and explain why – this is very important: You have to make sure that it is understood why you will not promise something, if you don't explain people might think you implicitly promised something that you didn't.

Unfortunately it is part of today's business world that people will try to force you into decisions and promises - be aware of that and don't accept it.

Doing the right thing, means adding product value

Doing the right thing outside of your work environment, is not an easy task. To do so highly depends on a high standard moral and belief system. However in business it is fairly simple to do the "right thing".

Just ask yourself one question:

"Is what I am doing right now, adding any value to our product?"

If you can't answer this question with a clear "Yes", than you are NOT doing the right thing. Stop immediately and find something more worthwhile to do.

Don't get confused by a company's mission statement, strategy or vision. These all imply that you have already made sure you do the right thing. Look for example at Google's "Do no evil" mission statement, this implies that employees should do "no evil", while doing the right thing – it does not necessarily mean you are doing the right thing by not doing evil! This is an important differentiation to make.

Any company is about adding value for their customer in whatever they do. If you don't add value, the customer has no incentive to buy your product or service. If too many parts of your organization are not contributing value to your product your service will be too expensive. That's how you lose customers.

Make it a habit to ask yourself at work, "Am I adding value to the final product?" Encourage everyone else to develop the same habit - especially your team members. Don't get stuck in "but we have always done it this way" or "this has always worked before" discussions.

If it doesn't add value, make sure it gets cut. Start with simple things like meetings. Meetings are one of the biggest sources for lost productivity in the workplace today.

Look at your schedule, and think about every single meeting invitation you received for the upcoming week: How many of those add value to the bottom line of your company?

How many of those could be done with fewer people? How many could be done in less time?

I am usually able to eliminate 60%-70% of all my meetings if I take a critical look at the topic, the decisions that will be made, the time-slot, and the other attendees that were invited.

This same critical thinking should go into every detail of your daily schedule.

Ensure that every task, every project and every meeting contributes to the bottom line - make sure that you only do the right things!

Eighty – Twenty

(Also known as the Pareto principle or the 80-20 rule)

"For many events, roughly 80% of the effects come from 20% of the causes"

I am sure many of you have heard about the eighty – twenty rule. In regards to efficiency it is based on the observation that the last 20 percent of a task require 80 percent of the time and effort (and many times budget).

This observation holds true for many other relationships in business such as:

• 80% of your revenue comes from 20% of your customers
• 80% of your profits come from 20% of the invested effort
• 80% of your complaints come from 20% of your customers
• 80% of your sales come from 20% of your products
• 80% of your innovations are made by 20% of your staff

This shows the vast areas of possible improvements by concentrating on the first 80% rather than the remaining 20%.

Still many managers want to be perfect. Reach one hundred percent in whatever they are doing – finish that task or project completely. These are your control freaks and perfectionists.

The problem with this approach is – it is not possible! You'll never have enough time to finish and reach those one hundred percent. There will never be enough time for the perfect product or the perfect project.

At any given time, you have many different tasks to prioritize and get done, people to supervise, disasters to avert. This is the reason why your job exists! You are a manager of scarce resources. Face it – if the perfect project, finished in time and budget, producing the best possible product would be possible – we wouldn't need managers.

Eighty percent sounds pretty good to me. Most of the time eighty percent is just enough. Those last twenty percent of polish and over engineering will cost you eighty percent of your time and budget. It is not worth it.

By following this concept you'll get much accomplished and will establish yourself as someone who "gets stuff done" in your organization. This is important for a leader. Complexity and Over engineering is your natural enemy – they bog you down and stop you from being efficient.

Complaints are good

If you've ever had someone complain to you, you might not agree with the title of this section. If you never had anyone complain to you - you don't listen very carefully!

Take a minute and think about it. If you yourself are not satisfied with a service or a product, what do you do?

Do you complain every single time?

Do you have the feeling someone takes you seriously if you complain?

Most of the times, we don't complain because it is too much effort and usually yields minimal returns.

What does that tell us about someone complaining to us? It means it is actually as much effort for him to complain, than it is for us to listen and take him serious. It is important that he feels we take him seriously. Otherwise he might never complain to you again. Why is this bad? Because, he will complain again to someone else! He will walk around and badmouth your product or service. This is the worst possible outcome, as there is by that point nothing you can do about it. He already complained to you before and you didn't take him seriously, why should he try again with you?

Change your mindset and take complaints as something positive:

Your customers or colleagues want to give you valuable business feedback.

Many use the term feedback as a better word for "complaint" but it doesn't change anything. At first, complaints will make you defensive, as we are usually attached to our products or services.

Don't be; accept that things go wrong in business. Accept that you yourself or your product might not be perfect. See this as an opportunity to get closer to perfection by listening carefully to the complaint and taking whatever action possible, depending on available resources. This might only be an acknowledgement of the complaint and acceptance that your product - designed and produced under the 80:20 principle - is not perfect and never will be.

And yes, there are unwarranted complaints from time to time, but these are the exception and not the rule. Ensure that you take every complaint seriously.

Measurement based Management

"If you can't measure it, you can't manage it."
(Robert S. Kaplan)

Many things in the business world can distract you from your goals. People will try to influence you or will be influenced by others, circumstances will change, projects will be stopped for reasons you cannot change and people will try to steal time from you either consciously or subconsciously.

On top of all these distractions you and your team members are human beings bringing their own ideas and – even worse – emotions into the picture.

All this will keep you busy and demand your full attention as manager. You need to juggle resources, tasks, sudden interruptions and important projects and people. The only way for you to do this successfully is to measure everything by facts and numbers.

Don't try to wing it – sooner or later you will lose.

Use some simple methods of keeping track of tasks and projects. Stay away from elaborate methods that create more work than the actual task of keeping track of things. I use simple email folders to keep track of tasks in my email Client. I do this because this is the one application that I know I have open all day. I tried spreadsheets, note taking applications, task managers and paper based versions of all the above – but in the end, I chose Microsoft Outlook because it gets out of my way and lets me focus on my actual work. Try out different methods and then pick the one that works best for you.

Define clearly - on a regular basis - your expectations. Not in a general way but very detailed and specific in numbers that everyone agrees to.

I recommend trying something I call "Measurement based Management" – this technique allows you and your employees reporting to you to define tasks and goals for the upcoming week. Write down the most important tasks on a whiteboard, at the end of the week come back together to check if all the tasks were completed or if something is still open. This can also be done in different time intervals, depending on the reliability of your staff and the nature of your work tasks. Sometimes a daily interval to start with makes more sense. If you use a method like this you will quickly understand the workload of your team and where there is potential for increased productivity and efficiency.

Do not accept apologies for a task not completed, instead request concrete facts and numbers why it wasn't done.

"I had so many other things to do." or "I was waiting for someone else." is not acceptable – make clear that you expect reasoning based on facts and numbers. What did he do instead? What other tasks interfered and were these completed? How long did he wait for someone else? Who was he waiting for and why?

If there are no clearly stated facts you must assume that your team is either not working efficiently, postponed the task because they didn't want to work on it, or your priorities were not understood clearly.

Either way, this needs to be rectified either by you directly, or the responsible team leader and that.

If you manage based on facts and numbers you'll be able to identify your top performers quickly. They usually do not postpone projects, base their to-do lists on the same priorities as you do and will not use excuses when it comes to under achievement but they will have an easy to understand fact based reason why things didn't go the way it was expected.

But then again, if they manage their projects based on facts and numbers most of the times they will achieve the set goals easily.

One more thing

So you are done for the day. Good for you. However, there is one more rule that you can apply universally to everything you do:

"Do one more thing! "

It doesn't matter what it is – just do it. It could be one more email or one more phone call - give yourself that extra motivational push by accomplishing just that one more thing.

I wrote this section as my "one more thing" one night before leaving the office – one less thing to tackle the next day, one more check on my to-do list.

Even more important for your success is that it will be one more thing than what everyone else does.

You will see how much you can accomplish just by following this simple rule every day.

Be organized

„Organized minds make successful people."

Being organized these days is harder than ever. You have more things to do every day, more tasks to track and just not the time to clean up. We kid ourselves that hundreds of unread emails in your inbox prove how important you are and your scattered desk demonstrates that you are very busy.

Keeping organized is a challenge and many tools we have these days like our iPads and Smartphones sometimes even make it harder. Multitasking has been proven to be much less effective in humans than in machines – the task loses our attention, and we end up not finishing several tasks at the same time.

However if you are not organized you will not be successful in what you are doing. This principle is independent of your job and your personality.

So I put together some easy ways of getting organized in today's corporate environment. Simple rules that you can apply individually and immediately.

Always work from a list

This might be one of the more obvious rules to follow as most of us already use some kind of self-organization, task management or to-do list approach.

However, surprisingly few people stick to it. They try constantly new ways of organizing themselves and lose sight of the goal. By trying out dozens of new task, project, and to-do management Apps, they soon realize they probably should put finding the right tools for self-organization on their to-do list!

If you already found your way of organizing yourself and it works well for you, keep on doing it. However if you have trouble getting things done, you keep finding yourself putting things off, or you just plain forget things, then make sure that from now on you work from a list.

A list is helpful in prioritizing your work. It can help you identify the most annoying task you have to do first thing in the morning and it will help you identify that other thing – the most important item on your task list for your manager.

It will also help you to focus throughout the day. You have to handle many disruptions every day and the list helps to keep your head free to deal with these minor or major disruptions without losing focus.

So how do you organize your list?

This is up to you. But make sure you do not start making this a complicated method of collecting everything you ever wanted to do. Focus on the day ahead of you – sit down in the morning and make the list. Do not start some elaborate task management system with days, weeks, months and years – this will only bog you down and frustrate you because there is still so much to do and let's face it, in your job all these tasks change continuously anyway.

Focus on this day – create your list in a simple way. If you want to use your smartphone for this – fine, as long as the App gets out of your way and makes it easy to work with the list. The only thing you actually have to do with the list is adding items during the day and checking items off as completed. I prefer to use a simple sheet of paper for this as it is the fastest and easiest way to manage my list.

When you first put down the list of things to do in the morning, take a brief moment and check if you can delegate any of them to your team members or direct colleagues – if so, great.

Delegation is one of your greatest tools to get ahead in your job so use it as often as possible. Don't bother keeping track if your tasks get done – just trust your people and make sure they know that you place this trust in them.

During the day make sure you mark tasks as completed as you go. This will give you a sense of accomplishment, motivate you and make you more focused on the remaining tasks on your list.

At the end of the day you should have completed all your tasks (like that ever happens…).

If you are like most managers there will be some tasks left – don't fret about it, this is easy to handle.

First, scratch all the tasks that have no more meaning if they are done by tomorrow. Then think about the remaining tasks – are they important or did you just put them down as reminders? Scratch them out if they are not important to you or your manager. Whatever task remains is a good candidate for the simple rule of "One more thing" – but even then you will still have tasks on your list that you must just leave for the next day.

So start a fresh list with these tasks for the next day and remember you will never get finished with everything you want to do anyway – get used to it.

Meetings

"If you had to identify, in one word, the reason why the human race has not achieved, and never will achieve, its full potential, that word would be: meetings."

(Dave Barry, "Things That It Took Me 50 Years to Learn")

Most Meetings in today's corporate culture are the biggest waste of time ever. People got so used to meetings that they use them as a placeholder for an actual social life. As if their motto is: "If you can't meet with friends arrange for a meeting at work".

Don't get me wrong – meetings are not evil, meetings in itself are not unnecessary; but the way we organize and manage meetings is just terrible.

Meetings are often too long, have no clear agenda, too many people are invited and the decision and action to be taken as the result of the meeting are not defined.

There are only two kinds of meetings you ever need to organize or attend:

First – hold a meeting to get a decision you cannot make on your own (for whatever reason).

If you don't have a decision to make where you need the agreement of others do not call a meeting! It is as easy as that.

If you need a meeting for agreement or support from others make sure that only those people are invited, don't accept delegation to non-decision makers from anyone you have invited. Ensure that before the meeting the goal of the meeting is clear; provide a fixed agenda and a suitable time slot. Very seldom is there the need for a meeting longer than 15 minutes. Don't accept the 30 minute default time slot that Microsoft Outlook offers you – arrange for exactly the amount of time you think you need – if it is 12 minutes make an invitation for 12 minutes (by the way, short meetings will ensure that people focus, are on time and actually show up).

Second – hold a meeting to get information (e.g. a project status or simply a review meeting)

Again only invite people who actually can contribute to the topic in question. If you have to invite more than three people the meeting will lose focus – try to split up if possible (even if this creates additional meetings for you). Make sure you let everyone you invited give you their information in a focused manner. Do not ask for "death by PowerPoint" (30 presentation slides in 30 minutes will put everyone in the room to sleep, guaranteed) but rather encourage more lively ways of presenting the current status, situation, progress etc.

Even for bigger projects do not hold meetings longer than one hour – it is better to meet on a regular basis and keep each meeting as short and focused on specific topics as possible. Do not let everyone present all the progress he has ever made – just the things that actual changed since your last meeting (see also "Don't tell your life story!").

A meeting should never be a platform for your team members or others to sell themselves - do not encourage show-off behavior.

Start every meeting on time! Do not accept the "let's wait 5 minutes rule" – that way you teach people that it is ok to be late to your meetings. Take 5 minutes after the meeting to prepare a quick email to all participants about the results and decisions taken – do not ask for corrections or amendments.

If for any reason a follow up meeting is necessary schedule it immediately with everyone there and make sure you have everyone's agreement.

Although some people might say that for common courtesy the following behaviors are not acceptable, you should stick to them to encourage everyone to be more focused and productive at work:

- If you are invited to meetings that are unfocused and are wasting your time speak up and make clear that you cannot accept this. Show that you are impatient.

- Even if you are not the organizer of a meeting do not accept late beginnings – take over the role of the moderator and start the meeting (you already know the agenda and points to discuss from the invitation, if not do not attend!).

Presentations

Being organized and efficient is even more important when it comes to presentations.

You will have to give many presentations along the course of your career. And the higher your position, the more frequent and important these presentations will become.

There are many things you won't be able to influence; maybe you always get stage fright when speaking in front of many people, maybe you have to present in a foreign language you don't feel a hundred percent comfortable in, or maybe presentations are just not your thing.

But please, do the one thing you can influence: perfect preparation!

No matter what kind of presentation you have to give, if you feel comfortable with the content or not - nothing is easier than to be perfectly prepared.

First of all - learn how to use PowerPoint or Keynote. Prepare your presentations yourself! Whenever possible do not give presentations prepared by someone else!

When you listen to someone else presenting you can usually spot immediately if the presentation was prepared by the presenter or someone else. I have seen the worst presentations with the presenter skipping ahead and back through his slide deck to try to understand the logic of the presentation he is giving -

do not do that and make sure you prepare your own presentations.

To be efficient in this, learn how to work with the application. Decide on your own presentation style if there is no corporate standard to follow - if there is a standard always use it, do not waste time by inventing your own presentation template.

To make the slides interesting remember that when it comes to presentations "less is more" - no colors, no animation, no "death by PowerPoint". The slides are a visual tool to accompany your speech - not a printout for the audience!

If you don't have your own style yet (maybe you are more of an introvert and therefore speaking in public is not your biggest joy) watch some presentations and try to discover what you like and what you would feel comfortable with.

Whatever you do, it has to be authentic! If you can copy Steve Jobs or Guy Kawasaki and it fits with your personality that's great, if it looks like an act or some kind of performance to your audience it will not help your presentation.

So make sure you are perfectly prepared, have the best slide deck you can build, feel comfortable and authentic in your presentation style and ensure all the technical aspects are checked beforehand (be there ahead of time, test the equipment, test your presentation file, etc.) and you will be able to make any presentation a success!

From Joe's world:

I have to admit that I have struggled my whole work life with giving presentations. I have a very introverted personality and do not enjoy being in the limelight. This trait has gotten in my way many times in my desire to be a successful manager.

I know that my presentation style is not my greatest strength, but I also know that I can easily convince people as long as my content is valid and the delivery of that content is well prepared. I make sure my slides are informative but not overloaded with information and that they support what I am saying rather than just reading them to the audience. I make sure that the presentation equipment is set up well ahead of time and that the configuration of the room makes it easy for me to connect with my audience instead of being separated by distance or other obstructions .

As a consultant early in my career, I was asked to give a presentation at a trade show about one of the projects I had worked on. I agreed not knowing that I would not be the one preparing the presentation. The project manager in charge had put together the slide deck in a hurry, basically copying from the project documentation. This resulted in far too many slides with no visually stimulating content, basically just sentence after sentence copied onto PowerPoint slides. I didn't spend enough time reviewing his slides and just assumed it would be alright. It wasn't.

It was hands down the worst presentation that I have ever given. I had to flip between slides just to understand myself what I was talking about, I never connected with the audience, people walked out on me and I received only negative feedback.

Since then, I have made it my rule not to present anything that I didn't prepare myself. If I must present one prepared by someone else, I always invest enough time reviewing it.

Don't tell your life story

Get to the point! That's it.

Don't waste everyone's time with chit-chat - just get to the point and get out.

Done!

Sometimes we tend to say too much. Either because you think it would be helpful to explain how you got to the decision you are presenting or because you just like your voice - either way, it is usually a waste of time for everyone in the room.

If you talk about a specific task or project make sure you focus on this - don't start with giving a general overview of what you are doing in your job. Everyone already knows! That's why people showed up in the first place - because they know what you are doing and that you are the right person for this task/project /decision.

So be positive, keep it short and give everyone else their time back!

From Joe's world:

My first meeting with the CEO of my company came about because I was responsible for a project that was not going well. Many people had complained to him and when meeting him I had the urge to explain what I am doing for the company, the background of the project and why our customers' perception of us was negative.

I knew people had complained and that the project's fast pace was making many unhappy. I believed in the project and was determined to power through. This was my first meeting with the CEO, I had just gotten hired and I wanted to make sure he understood all this.

His reaction was simple. He basically told me to shut up! He already had all the facts he wanted, he knew we had to keep going and he knew I was the right person to finish the project successfully. All he wanted was a rough estimate of how long it would take.

I did shut up, told him 2 more weeks and stopped telling my "life story". (I am proud to say, we did end up finishing the project which transformed the IT infrastructure of our company on schedule.)

Zero Inbox

Keep your inbox clean! Your physical as well as your electronic inbox.

By the end of your day – every day – you must have zero items in your inbox. Everything else is procrastination which will end up in inefficiency, delays, redundant work and demotivation.

Make sure you touch every inbox item only once – especially with email and our current way of working using Mobile Devices to read and response to email we tend to touch inbox items several times. We read on our mobile device, decide it is too hard to answer (maybe due to the form factor of that device), we move it to a folder or leave it marked as read in our Inbox just so that we will read it again – possibly with lower priority – on our Computer, or forget about it because we have already filed it away.

If you open and read an email on your mobile device – make sure you answer and delete it.

Do not skim through with any action – there is little to no benefit in this. Later, when you get to your desk, you will spend the same amount of effort to read the same message again. If you touch an item make sure you handle it and get done with it!

Many of us get more than 100 emails every day – there is no way you will be able to read all of them and act upon each of them.

If you leave them in your Inbox, there is no way you will do anything about them later!

You have to make sure your Inbox is empty at the end of the day. Don't create an elaborate Folder structure for emails to be handled later – filing and finding them again will take too much effort. If you don't do it now, you won't do it later.

If an email concerns something you cannot do now because you have to wait for a later date (maybe you have to get some information first or wait for a strategic decision) then change the email into an appointment and delete it.

All emails that you get in copy (cc) delete automatically or file away automatically. Everything that is in your Inbox at the end of the day – delete! Don't convince yourself that these mails are too important to delete and that you'll handle them by tomorrow – you won't!

If they were flagged as important by the sender – you would have handled them right away. If they were important and not flagged by the sender as important – believe me, he will send it again if he wants an answer from you!

Now you've learned how to start your day with a clean Inbox (besides the mails you got overnight from business partners in different time zones). This will help you to be much more effective and motivated every day.

Now – we have to discuss some exceptions to this rule. Do not delete messages from your manager, his or her manager or anyone above that. This exception is easy enough to put into automatic rules of your email client. Ensure that these messages – even when sent in copy – will not be deleted or filed away. Mark them as important so that you immediately see them at the end of the day, before you delete all remaining items in your inbox.

Remember – never touch an item twice. When you receive an important message and open it, you must act upon it and promptly delete it. Do not file it, print it or, put it in a "To Do pile" (which you should not have anyway).

Inbox management is an important topic in a manager's workday these days because it's one of the greatest distractions to a productive day. Do not create a filing cabinet inside your Mailbox (todays search engines in email clients find anything – filing is unnecessary and a waste of your time). Try to set aside specific times during the day where you actually work on your open emails. Live the Zero Inbox Policy and delete everything before you leave the Office.

At least once a year delete everything in your Mailbox that is older than 13 month: I usually do this just before the Christmas break.

There is no reason to keep older email communications. Everything older than 13 months has no value anymore. However, if it is business relevant communication, archive it (by business relevant I mean legal documents like invoices, offers, etc.).

Clean Up!

"A cluttered desk is a sign of a cluttered mind."

You might disagree with this and believe that a cluttered desk or work environment is a sign of genius, creativity and self-expression. It's not.

It is a sign of inefficiency, laziness and bad manners.

If your office looks like a garbage dump, it doesn't matter if you can prove that you could find anything that you are being asked for in less than 5 minutes - it still looks like a garbage dump!

First of all it is not "your" office - it's your company's office and therefore represents your company. Don't make your office an extension of your living room. It is a place to work, not a place where you express yourself and try to show off your personality. If you need to do that write a book or start painting.

Second, no matter how much you personally believe in chaos theory - it is not efficient. This goes back to the basic rule of "touch every item only once" that I have already discussed in the "zero inbox" section.

If your desk is cluttered with paper (and even worse with all kinds of other stuff) you will, even if you intend otherwise, touch many items more than once. You won't finish necessary tasks and you will waste time. You read a document - maybe just half of it - and put it back on the pile. You will inevitably read the beginning of the same document over and over again until you remove it from your desk.

Don't just keep it there - read it (if you must), act on it, get rid of it!

At the end of the day you should have an empty desk or at least a neat desk knowing exactly what to start with the next day.

Do not start a "mystery pile", "to do later", "read when I have time" etc. - you will never do it, mess up your desk, distract yourself with all the stuff you still have to do and sooner or later get demotivated because there is no way you ever get done.

Besides your cluttered desk also take care of the rest of your office - there is no reason why your office should not look perfectly organized and clean every day. Don't store stuff in your office, don't get more and more shelves for all your "important" stuff.

I believe in the zero cabinet office - I have one small container for personal files (that can be locked) - and that is all.

No additional papers, no folders, no stuff.

Be you!

„In order to be someone, you must first be yourself."

Whoever you are - be yourself. Especially at work! Don't play a role, don't try to copy someone else and don't change your personality the minute you walk into your office.

Just be the same person you are for the rest of your life, with your family, your friends at home or at church.

If you are open and blunt - be open and blunt. Don't try to mellow down. If you are quite, don't try to be dramatic for show at work. People see through it if you play a role - be yourself, accept the way you are and don't apologize for it.

I don't think I ever really minded that I define myself in big parts through my work. I don't go to work, I work! And this is not meant in an arrogant or prideful way – I don't think I necessarily work longer or harder than anyone else. I truly believe it is wrong to separate your time on the job from the rest of your day or the rest of your life.

If your work is not a part of your life you can embrace and enjoy you are doing it wrong!

I am very well aware that this does not fit our current culture, even more so in the less capitalistic societies like Europe. Unions and Workers Councils define themselves through regulation of working time and the separation of work and free time (the so called work-life balance).

But again – if your main goal is to ensure a strict separation of the thing you are doing for most of your awake time in life and the rest of it

a.   You should change your job and attitude towards it and

b.   You are reading the wrong book.

Insecure managers create complexity

(Jack Welch)

This is a simple truth – not just for managers.

Whenever we are insecure about something we start to create complexity. We design elaborate processes to be followed, define documentation guidelines or just simply create complex products. We are unfocused when insecure about a topic. We tend to make it more complex, look at all the possible problems instead of the solution. In the end, we create inefficiency or just a really ugly and un-useful product.

Insecure managers tend to build an elaborate organization, detailed processes without added value, confusing reporting lines and many times misinformation. You can spot them easily whenever you hear, "This is too complex, and we cannot tackle this right now!"

Never trust anyone who claims he is taking care of something so complex that it cannot even be discussed! There is no such thing.

A secure manager will always be able to tell you exactly what he or she and their organization is doing, how he or she is benefitting the company, and why these specific tasks are necessary for the final outcome. Do not hide behind complexity. Complexity is not valuable (even though people sometimes think so) - simplicity is the real value.

Only if your organization is simple, your team members know what they are contributing to the bottom line and why they are doing what they've been told to – only then you are really doing your job as a manager. Even more important – only then can you rise to the top because you have people on your team who will be able to take over responsibility from you and follow you when you are going on to the next level.

Do not underestimate this - it is very important as many times you might not get promoted if your manager believes that your role is too critical to manage the complexity you have created and there is no one from your team or from elsewhere in the organization who could take over your responsibility.

So don't be insecure – be bold, learn everything you need to know for your current position, foster a team of high performers you can rely on, delegate responsibility and make yourself available for the next step by avoiding complexity in all areas.

Don't network – Work!

Many people will tell you that to be successful as a manager you have to build up a network and spend much of your time maintaining this network.

I disagree with this notion and believe that networking for the most part is a waste of your time!

Instead of spending hours and hours at business lunches, informal meetings, pre-meetings or even drinking coffee with co-workers, managers and people completely unrelated to your position -you should just work.

You will get so much more work done than the managers who spend half their time networking. This real work will shine through when it comes to reviewing your performance and contribution.

Networking can replace hard work at the beginning of your career. It is easy to move up in the organization as long as your relative responsibility is low. As soon as your contribution to the organization becomes visible however, networking will not help you to get ahead. You will be judged by your work and not your "friend status".

And while we are at it – social networking based on popular services like Facebook or Twitter are as much a waste of your time as real life networking. Just don't do it!

Some of these social networking tools might be helpful to organize your contacts or aggregate relevant industry news – but make sure that this is how you are using them. If you start sharing your favorite YouTube videos, funny presentations and other unnecessary status updates you are wasting your time and don't get anything in return.

Use a more professional oriented service like LinkedIn or Plaxo for organizing your contacts and use Twitter as a news aggregator by following the news outlets that are important to your current job role (this never ever includes the "Joke of the Day").

Use these tools only when necessary – if you have found a better system for contacts and news aggregation, use that system.

Remember that whatever you publish on any of these services is by definition public. It will be read by your team members, your manager, your future employer and everybody else.

All this said I believe it is important not to confuse networking with healthy relationship building.

Remember at work, you should strengthen the relationships with these three important groups:
- Your manager

- Your direct reports

- Your top performers

These are the people that will get you ahead because they either support you with their own hard work or because they directly judge your performance.

Make sure you take some time out of your busy schedule and ensure that you are on the same page with these three important groups of people at work. They must understand your motivation and your goals so that they are able to follow you (remember they also want to follow the rule: "Do that other thing" – this they can only do, when they understand what you expect of them).

Don't go to any social events at work if you can avoid it. Go to the ones that you organize yourself for your team, but leave early. Go if your boss invites you, but leave early. Whenever you have an all hands event and you don't have to give a speech or presentation – don't go. Spend your social time with the important people in your life (your family, your friends) and keep a professional relationship with your co-workers and employees.

Don't network – just work!

Work is what I do

Almost all of us still live and work today as we did two hundred years ago during the industrial revolution.

We have entered the information age but ignored many of the changes that come with it. We like the way we work because we are so accustomed to it. But are we productive? Is our style of work effective? There are many who would reason that we are indeed a lot more productive then we were one or two generations ago – and this is in some aspects true. However, I believe if we want to evolve further, if we want to push efficiency and productivity to new levels – not just incremental but exponential – we need to change the way we work and transform the workplace wherever possible.

And this starts with a simple insight:

Work is what you do - not a place you go to.

When most people go to work they are confronted with all the traditions of the modern workplace. They clock-in, fill out time recording sheets and make sure that every single minute is accounted for.

If you do this long enough (we as a society have done this long enough) the definition of work becomes time you spend at a place called work. If that is our view we are all doomed. By that I don't mean something horrible will immediately happen to society, but I do strongly believe that if we keep being stuck in our old ways of work, we will in the end lose any productivity gains we have accomplished in the past. We will begin to stagnate in our evolution.

Worst of all, this mindset creates an unbelievably demotivated workforce. We produce employees who will show up every day for the allotted amount of time and produce next to nothing. Why do they produce next to nothing? Because that is exactly what we have asked them to do!

We do not encourage a task based, goal oriented style of work. Every Entrepreneur is goal oriented and not a time clock puncher. Nobody pays them for time, just results. If there are no results, they are out of money.

Payment for results is a very simple but unbelievable powerful encouragement. Unfortunately, this concept is only understood by a very small percentage of our workforce today. Everyone else gets paid no matter what they do as long as they show up on time! (I understand I am oversimplifying here quite a bit, and there are many shades of grey in between this black and white scenario).

We need to change the way we run our businesses, in order to encourage and manage our employees and ensure that we fulfill the promises that the information age brings with it. How can we do this? Quite simple, we must embrace a new definition of work:

Work is what you do – not a place you go to!

Putting this into practice is one of the biggest managerial challenges you will face in a big corporation today. This means you have to manage based on results – this will demand clearly defined objectives that are well understood by your employees (and agreed upon). It will replace the general notion of "I clock in, therefore I am!"

As soon as you have transformed your organization to work result based (instead of time measurement based), you will be able to continuously increase productivity and employee satisfaction. If done correctly employees will achieve a feeling of accomplishment with the realization that suddenly it really pays off to do their job in the most efficient way!

This is crap!

Well, here we are. I said it – this is crap!

How many times a day do you hear this at work? How many times did your manager, your colleagues or your team members confront you with "This is crap!"?

If your organization is like mine, this has happened approximately ZERO times over the last 10 years and won't happen any time in the near future either (with the noteworthy exception of one single manager, who frequently used the "Shit" version of this phrase and achieved surprisingly great results across his whole part of our organization).

I've seen this reluctance to truth many times and it really bothers me. Believe me; everyone knows when they see shit!

Everyone thinks to themselves, "This is shit!" but tries to evade this blatant criticism by saying "Hmmm, it looks pretty good already – why don't you work another week on it and come back to me?"

You know what is a lot more productive for everyone involved? I think you figured it out.

We have to encourage everyone we are working with to be blatantly honest! If something is great, call it great – if something is shit, call it shit!

There is no politically correct way of saying it without creating mixed messages or a huge loss in productivity.

If you label something "ok", and encourage your team members to tweak it a little bit more, you not only waste your own time, but also the valuable resources of your whole team. The end result will be: "ok shit".

If you tell it like it is, you will have a positive influence on your team and the quality of whatever you are producing.

No expectations – no disappointments

Sounds pretty cynical, doesn't it?

The point is you really should have no expectations towards anyone at work! Otherwise, you will be disappointed sooner rather than later.

Don't get me wrong, you should definitely state your expectations regarding goal fulfillment, project milestones, behavior, and company culture clearly. The more often you do this, the better. Make sure everyone completely understands what you expect from them. But do not expect anything without communicating it!

You have to realize that most people you work with are driven by other interests than yourself. You set yourself up for a huge disappointment if you think everyone around you wants to do their best for the goals of your team, project or company.

That is just not the case. Most people go to work because they need the money. Their motives are much different from yours. Don't ever assume that you are motivated in the same way as anyone else in your company and therefore your goals and methods will be the same. More often than not, you realize too late that this is not the case and you are aiming straight for disaster. You expected too much from your team or your project members without stating your expectations **specifically**.

So help yourself and avoid disappointments, don't just expect stuff to happen!

Be authentic

In today's business environment this is easier said than done. Sometimes it seems almost everyone is straight out of drama class and playing some kind of role at work.

I get annoyed at co-workers or managers that pretend they are someone else at work than they are in real life. Get over it! You are not fooling anyone – don't try to play smart by throwing around buzzwords and talking about things you clearly know nothing about. I know it's hard, because in the business environment you probably never get called on it – nobody will ever say to you "stop talking shit!" – But be assured people notice, even if you are good at it.

Over time everyone will notice that you are not being yourself.

Not being authentic will lead to inconsistency in your management style and your relations with your team – so stop doing it.

If people tell you that some of your behavior irritates them or that you should act differently in the business world, you of course should question yourself and check if the behavior is generally acceptable. But, in the end don't try to hide personality traits and character – it will not work and inconsistency will irritate everyone around you even more.

So be who you are – be authentic, embrace your own style and expect the same from others.

Remember that if you behave in any other way people will always notice (maybe not at first – but sooner or later they will). This is dangerous because people automatically start to treat a "pretender" with mistrust and question anything he or she does.

Don't bring this fate upon yourself. Being authentic and not playing a role are a part of character and integrity, which are as important at work as they are at home with your family and friends.

Integrity

Integrity as a business manager requires consistency in everything you do.

You are the most important behavioral example for your team and your company. If you become inconsistent in your values, not authentic in your actions, and your way of treating your people results from favoritism or unfairness, you will lose your leadership role very, very quickly.

Others in your organization will copy your behavior and this will result in subpar performance. Don't expect highly motivated employees if you don't show integrity in everything you do. Only then will people see you as a real leader. Fair treatment, equal measures and principles will ensure you'll be viewed as a reliable leader who deserves loyalty from his colleagues and subordinates.

Especially when difficult and uncomfortable decisions have to be made (layoffs, benefit cuts, etc.) you must always show integrity and stay the course. The smallest sign of evading tough decisions, favoring certain employees or being inconsistent will be seen as weakness and shady behavior – and rightly so.

Having integrity is one of the most difficult things to do in today's business environment – you will be tested every day. It is of utmost importance that you pass these tests.

Real leaders always show integrity (at work and at home) and are always acting as an example for their whole organization!

From Joe's world:

In every manager's life you get to the point when you have to let someone go. Unfortunately, most of the time this is not based on the employee's bad performance, but on companywide cost cutting or restructuring inside the organization.

I once had to deal with this situation and explain to one of my team members that I was letting him go due to cost cutting. I really struggled to not water down the message giving him false hope. I had worked with him for several years, so it was very hard to not get emotionally involved while I explained to him the reasons why he would be fired, making clear that there was no other way.

At the time, I wished I could tell him that we could find something else for him to do or that there might be a position for him elsewhere in the company. But I knew that showing favoritism and being inconsistent (to cut cost was mandatory) would reflect poorly on myself as a leader, and would have many negative implications for my team in the future.

There is no such thing as a good compromise in business.

Compromises lead to faulty products, lengthy discussions about what should have been and postponed project milestones.

Business is not a democracy. It is not a dictatorship either, as people are free to leave and pursue their personal goals elsewhere.

For the most part business is based on hierarchical organizations and chains of command. And this for good reason – don't fall in the trap of shared responsibility and accountability, don't start committees to make decisions – none of that will hold when it comes down to assessing your leadership capabilities.

If you want to be a manager, you have to prove it by leading.

This means you can delegate almost all of your work, but you can never delegate responsibility and accountability for your decisions.

To be able to stand behind your decisions they have to be ultimately yours and not the joined decision of a committee.

Compromise will always dilute your vision and your strategy. You will be influenced by others and lose your leadership role. At the end you'll lose authenticity and your team will stop following your lead.

Make sure you listen to everyone's viewpoint and use a democratic process for collecting views and ideas in order to come to your conclusion. But the decision is yours to make and you will be held accountable for it. The only compromise can be to do it your way!

Share everything!

At work share everything you do, know or own (for example resources). When you share you foster a work environment of collaboration and teamwork. You and your department will be seen as enablers and you will contribute much more to your company's success than you would holding back.

This is contradictory to the widespread "Information is power" mentality – but believe me – that mentality is PG (pre Google) and in today's business environment irrelevant.

If you don't share your information people will get it elsewhere without much effort. You will be seen as a hindrance to your company's success.

The same is valid for sharing resources. Don't build your empire based on headcount – don't cling to people. If they are needed in other projects or even departments ensure they are used to the maximum benefit of the company – not your own benefit.

Openness and sharing will always reflect positively on you and your entire team. It ultimately gets you more important projects and more possibilities to shine as a leader; your colleagues will trust and support you and will become important allies later when needed.

Have fun

"Choose a job you love, and you will never have to work a day in your life."

(Confucius)

There is nothing wrong with having fun at work. On the contrary, it improves the productivity of your team!

However, you cannot make your colleagues and team members have fun. Fun at work should stem from the success your team is creating. Being part of a successful team will inspire people and bring enjoyment to their work. It will become fun to be there.

Whenever people believe what they are doing is worthwhile, useful, challenging and interesting, they will have fun.

You as a manager can work on these intangibles and provide the right environment to make work fun. Don't try to force it by turning your workplace into an episode of "The Office" - just make sure that your people enjoy what they are doing. If you never see your coworkers laugh, if they try to get out of the building as fast as they can or are generally downtrodden at work, you are not doing your job and you are hurting your results!

Don't get me wrong, every job has a boring aspect to it. A fun task done a hundred times becomes boring. There is no job that is always just fun.

I love being a manager because of the product development part of my job. It gives me great freedom in decision making and the joy to work with the newest technology available. But I also have to do Reports, Budgets and mind-blowingly boring meetings. It is part of my job; I focus on it and get it over with as fast as possible, in order to get back to the fun part!

I see it as my job as manager to empower my people to act the same way. To help them enjoy what they are doing, and give them the right tools to do the things they do not enjoy as efficiently as possible. It is my task to create an environment in which my people understand the purpose of what they are doing (also the non-fun parts), have as much freedom as possible, and give them the feeling that they can count on me and each other. Then the fun comes naturally.

Fun at work has an added benefit as well. Along with fun, your people will be more creative and collaborative. Absenteeism and sick days will go down. In conclusion it is very much worth your while for you as a manager to foster a fun work environment. Here is what you need to do:

- Explain to your people what they are requested to do and why. How are they benefiting the bottom line? What is their contribution? Treat your people like adults by telling them the truth (see also "Be authentic" and "Integrity").
- Support your people. Give them what they need for their daily job. Make unpleasant processes as efficient as possible.

- Allow them the same freedom that makes your job fun. Give them time to be creative, try new things, understand and solve problems in new and unique ways.

With creating an environment that values creativity, critical thinking and success you enable your people to have fun, enjoy coming to work every day and be more invested in their job and in return in your success!

Be a manager

„Much has been said and written about a manager's need to be a leader. The fact is no single managerial activity can be said to constitute leadership, and nothing leads as well as example"

Andrew S. Grove

Being a good manager means achieving your goals and the goals of your company with fewer resources than you would actually need to do so.

This might not be the "official" definition but let's face it - that's what you really do every day and why you get paid more than other people!

To do this, you need to be able to set an appropriate framework for your people to work in and to push them to their top efficiency.

But as your resource is also limited you need to understand where to focus your energy and where to just accept mediocrity for the time being - if you are able to do this and get the best out of your people on the way you will rise to the top of your organization quick and easy.

Let me make that more clear: Never say "No!" to your Boss.

Because we like to treat everyone equal and be nice all around this rule usually starts a debate.

You might say I can say "No!" even to my direct manager – it is not a problem because "we have that kind of relationship".

No - you don't!

You should always say "Yes!" to your boss – it doesn't even matter what the request is (as long as it does not interfere with what I have said about integrity). It could be something that you believe should be addressed to a different team, something that is definitely not your area of expertise, something ridiculous or not work related at all.

Just try to understand, whatever it is you need to say "Yes!"

The simple reason for that is that even if you believe it is something you should decline, your boss specifically chose you – and no one else – to handle this problem for him.

Trust me when I say: your boss knows very well that it shouldn't be addressed to you, or that it is ridiculous, doesn't make sense or is not even work related. When I got asked to cancel my boss's gym membership, what do you think I answered?

The important thing to take away from this is that your boss just made you his go-to guy and that is all that matters to you!

Afterwards it is up to you how to follow through. You can delegate the task at hand, do it yourself, or outsource it – it doesn't matter as long as it gets done.

Make sure you follow up on it and keep your manager informed about the status at all times, remember this is important to him (this might be a good candidate for your daily "do that other thing").

Choose your battles

In your day to day operational work you will have many decisions to make and many battles to fight. Many times we can get emotionally involved and don't behave rationally anymore just because we want our point of view to prevail.

Don't step into this trap – you are at work, its business not private! Make sure you choose your battles wisely – you don't need to win every battle – you don't even need to fight every battle.

Look at every decision, every possibly controversial topic and decide for yourself:

- Is this a "must win" situation?

- Could this be a "quick win"?

- Is this an "easy win"?

If the situation fits any of these three scenarios you do want to fight and win – otherwise just step away and let someone else invest his time and effort.

A "must win" is easy to spot. Any decision, task, or project that is directly connected to your immediate success is a "must win" for you. Fight for these as hard as possible with all your resources and influence. Only do this if you are sure you can win (if you know from the onset you won't be able to win, don't get involved).

A "quick win" is usually a smaller project, decision or task that will help you be successful in the long run. It shows that you can be pragmatic by taking small steps to a bigger goal and will deter others from fighting with you over the long-term goal because you already have taken successful steps into that direction. (No one ever argues with success).

Always take an "easy win". It doesn't need much effort; you don't really need to fight anyone for it and it will establish you as a successful influencer and winner type in your company.

Choose your battles! Fight to win! Step away if you know you won't be able to succeed – there will be another day. And whatever you do try to not get emotionally invested!

Are you working hard at making yourself indispensable? If so, stop!

There is no value in being indispensable or rather in feeling as though you are indispensable. There is a lot of work in it for you and a lot of frustrations for others but, believe me; it adds no career value to you or added benefit for your company.

If you feel indispensable (and perhaps you are indispensable in some specific way), you force your company and your team to stop working when you're gone. You just made a huge mistake.

Let me tell you a little bit from my own experience:

When I started my last job, I worked 14 hours a day. I felt like I really contributed to the success of the company. I took all important projects and tasks because that was the most efficient way of performing. However – as soon as I went on vacation or on a business trip, my team fell apart.

It was so common that we already talked about it beforehand because we all knew it would happen. "Oh, you are gone next week? I guess the first disaster will hit by Monday morning".

Why?

Because I made myself indispensable by not sharing responsibility, not delegating critical tasks and worst of all - I felt good about it! ("Guess how important I am – the company can't run without me!").

The only problem with this work ethic is that you are not being more efficient, you are actually hurting your team and restricting others (usually your most important people). Sooner or later, you will kill your career.

That sounds a little bit over the top – doesn't it? After all, if you are indispensable how would that kill your career?

It's very simple; you are indispensable where you are right now.

There is no way anyone will give you a different role in your organization. You get stuck, passed over – do you still feel good about being indispensable?

So what you need to do is simple – empower your team. Delegate responsibilities freely, don't hold back knowledge (see also "Share"), encourage your team members or colleagues to take risks and work on becoming completely replaceable.

When you have reached that stage you are open for your next career step without your team or your company suffering. Only then will your direct manager even consider giving you a new opportunity as he will never create a situation where you leaving creates more work for himself.

I've seen many colleagues get stuck in "indispensable limbo" – their career going nowhere. In the end, they have to leave the company when it became clear that they were not indispensable, just stuck in their position. Imagine that, a couple of weeks later their team worked fine without them.

Motivation

I know there is plenty to be said about motivation. Complex, psychological explanations of what it is, how we can get it, and how we could motivate our team.

I firmly believe that most of that is – let's say it kindly –not true.

The most important truth is:

Only you can motivate yourself!

You might be thinking, "That's not true. A lot of things motivate me, and many of them are not under my direct control. What about the money I earn - the most profound source of motivation?"

Of course many forms of motivation exist, but they are only the framework – you create the motivation for yourself.

To create the motivational framework is your task as manager!

You have to ensure that the basic needs of your team members are met.

This includes responsibility, diversity, a desired work environment and of course, money. But it is only a framework – it looks different for each individual. Many times you assume by giving out more money you can motivate someone – this is true in the short term but a month later the salary increase or bonus is forgotten and with it the inherent motivation.

Don't misunderstand me – money is motivating to a certain extent. Most people go to work to earn a decent salary. If you ask your team if they come to work just to spend their time doing something interesting, how many of them do you think would say "yes"?

First and foremost they need to earn money. This is a basic need. But they also have other needs like responsibility for their work, autonomy for as many decisions as possible, and yes, self-fulfillment. But this - again - is just the framework that you have to provide.
To become top performers your people have to be able to motivate themselves. This is an important character trait – you should be looking for this in people because it is something you cannot provide, teach or substitute with anything else.

Only people who know how to self-motivate will be top performers. These are the workers you want around you because the better your team performs the better you perform.

So make sure the framework is right (and it probably will be different for every one of your team members) and look for the top performers that constantly motivate themselves without any external action by you or others.

These are the people you want to invest in, they are as important to your future as your own actions.

More importantly: Invest in the right people!

This might run counter to what you have heard before, but the right people are your top performers. Don't invest the majority of your time in the laggards – they don't deserve your attention. You won't be able to change them into top performers anyway (see also "People change").

You can't motivate them because they cannot motivate themselves. So don't try. It's a waste of your time and attention – give them the ten percent they deserve.

Focus the other ninety percent of your attention on your top performers. Coach them, give them feedback and enable them – they are able to motivate themselves and will even improve their performance if you give them the right framework.

If you have identified the right people to invest in, make sure you stick to it – these are the ones in your team that you will need for your future in the organization. They will be your personal support network after you have left for your next career step.

If you have top performers and have invested a lot of time and effort in their development, make sure you either keep them in your team or you place them in strategic positions inside the organization to enlarge your support network. Usually they will be thankful for your support and will help you later when you need it.

Don't confuse this with networking – networking is a complete waste of time. In this case you build loyalty based on trust and performance. Networking wastes your time with chit-chat and brown-nosing. You will never be sure if you can rely on those people in critical situations.

Make sure you invest in the right people!

Donuts

Free donuts always help!

If your team has a hard day in front of them with tough meetings or projects you need to finish bring some donuts for everyone.

You will see a mood change immediately – people open up, work harder and start collaborating. Sharing food always breaks the ice in workgroups – use this to your advantage with very little effort on your part. You will be surprised with the result.

The times they are a-changin'

"If your time to you is worth savin'
Then you better start swimmin'
Or you'll sink like a stone
For the times they are a-changin'."

(Bob Dylan)

People are generally afraid of change!

It is part of our nature. However, if you want to succeed as a manager you have to change! You have to change yourself every day, anticipate change in your business environment and be able to embrace that change. If you are not able to do that, the change will roll over you and leave you behind.

Change is always positive!

This is of course hard to believe, but if you are part of the change you will always come out on top. If your business environment changes and you have to make adjustments, it is of utmost importance that you do not try to fight the change.

There will be enough people who want to keep things the way they always were – don't be one of them.

How do you learn to embrace change and even more importantly, bring about change when necessary? There is no easy way that transforms you into a change agent. You must want to change, be open for change and not being protective of your way of doing things.

There are some excellent books on "change management" – I prefer Kotters' "Our iceberg is melting" as a good introduction on how to manage change in an organization.

To foster the attitude of "change is good" in your organization, make sure your team is not getting set in certain ways of doing things. It might sound unnecessary, but I believe that small changes, constantly triggered by you as a manager, can prepare your team to weather any "perfect change storm".

Make sure that your team members do not get attached to their physical surroundings – changing the office setup, seating arrangements, schedules etc. can help. The office should never become the extension of somebody's living room!

Next, make sure that you change your organization on a regular basis – once a year is a good time interval to keep everyone flexible. Change managers, areas of responsibility and reports around. This will ensure that everyone is prepared for even bigger changes and will keep your team members motivated as they gain more responsibility or just diversify their tasks.

With a team that is used to change on a daily basis you will be able to take on any major change that comes your way and remain effective even in times of crisis, when many around you stumble.

And believe me - change will come!

People change

Not!

You might disagree with me, but I firmly believe in this simple fact – people fundamentally do not change.

Much of our management wisdom is based on how we can change our workers – make them more efficient, productive and innovative.

Fact is – they won't! People follow their own desire; they will not be changed by you. If you have someone in your group who is highly motivated and productive but not very innovative, don't waste your time on trying to change him.

Take his or her good qualities and use these for the goals of your team – and find someone else who has good ideas!

If someone in your team is lazy, not trustworthy or in any other way disruptive to the team and your goals – get rid of him. You will not change him and you will waste too much of your scarce time trying.

Remember to invest your time in your top performers – not in your laggards. Get rid of the laggards. An organization can only take so many B-players until it goes down – make sure they are not in your team.

You want A-players so you have to hire A-players. Don't take anyone else –even if it's your only choice. If you can't hire who you want, don't take on laggards from inside your organization just to fill a position and increase your headcount (and that's all it will be – not a resource, just a headcount).

Your team will become poisoned by B-Players. They don't just waste their own time but also your A-Players time. Don't think you can take on anyone and change them – you won't.

Let them run dry

Many times in your professional career you will run into conflicts. Conflicts are not necessarily bad and can act as a catalyst to achieve something great together.
However, you will also have your fair share of conflicts resulting from emotional distress (either based on your own issues or someone else's.)

There are many ways of handling stress and conflict at work and if you have been a manager for a while you have probably taken part in one or more „conflict resolution" seminars or similar titled events. It is hard to learn how to deal with conflict and not to get emotionally invested. My preferred approach is just to let it happen. As I have stated above, conflict can be something very positive – it can resolve underlying issues and help you and your business partners actually be able to work together again in a productive way.

A smoldering conflict without a resolution will poison the atmosphere at work. It will ultimately result in lower morale and motivation.

Let the conflict happen and do not get emotionally involved yourself. This ensures that you stay in control of the situation and are able to steer the resolution into a positive direction.

This is a method I call „Let them run dry". Let them get out all of their anger and misgivings. Give everyone else time to vent until they literally run dry. This might take some time but do not interfere. When everyone gets rid of their underlying issues you can go ahead and tackle the real problem based on facts and figures.

The importance here is not to make the mistake of getting emotionally involved. Let them run dry, but don't take it personally. It's just their opinion.

From Joe's world:

I once had a very stressful time at work where I got into constant conflicts with a fellow manager. The issue seemed not to be rooted in actual problems, but rather a fundamentally different approach to managing our teams which resulted in mistrust and animosity between team members. Where my team members acted as autonomously as possible, he preferred a much more formal and hierarchical style. For a long time, I was not able to resolve the conflict until one day we were able to get together for coffee and I let him vent his anger. To my surprise, much of his frustration wasn't even directed towards me but instead to personal career issues he was dealing with. After he had had plenty of time to vent what had been bothering him, we were able to actually address the real issues between our teams. We have been close allies ever since, working very productively together.

Act first – apologize later

I told you that some of the ideas presented in this book will make you successful, not popular. This one definitely belongs in that category!

Many times I have observed how good ideas that would benefit an organization greatly if implemented in a timely manner, got killed by management indecisiveness or just plain inefficiency in the decision making process.

More than once I have seen how a great project falls apart because everyone wants to be responsible in making key decisions, but nobody wants to be accountable for them. It is important for them to be part of as many project steering committees as possible, and be at every meeting but not actually getting anything done. Projects take too long, the project organization gets bloated and in the end a great idea turned into something no one wants to be connected to anymore.

Project organization is necessary to run a project smoothly - but don't exaggerate. Keep the organization simple and when you get to the critical implementation steps be pragmatic - act first and apologize later.

You will soon realize that most of the time, you only have to apologize so that everyone can "save face". If you do act first, make sure you will be able to reach your goal; otherwise you set yourself up for a disaster. But if you are certain you can achieve your goal and that following the "correct" procedures will take too, ignore standard procedure and go for it.

As I mentioned, you will have to apologize for this. But, your success will prove you right. Remember, as a manager you are ultimately accountable for reaching your goals.

Acting first will earn you the image of one who gets stuff done. This is much more important to your career than playing nice (Warning: If you do this, some jealous , weaker coworkers will say that your success has not been earned as you did not follow proper procedure and ignored them in the decision making process).

I do this at work every day. So much so that I calculate in an apology beforehand.

Delegate

"Surround yourself with the best people you can find, delegate authority, and don't interfere as long as the policy you've decided upon is being carried out."

(Ronald Reagan)

Delegation is one of your most important tools as a manager.

When you have reached the point where you can delegate everything you have to do in your daily job, you are free to completely focus on your next career step.

You have also greatly empowered your direct reports and given them the same chance of moving to the next level (Yours!). If you don't get ahead, they don't get ahead. You will always be in a mutually beneficial coexistence with your direct reports, as long as you give them as much responsibility as possible.

There is no benefit in holding back anything. Sure there will always be tasks that you want to do yourself, either because they are of importance or simply because you were asked to do them yourself. Do not delegate those tasks. You will also have tasks and decisions based on confidential information that you will not be able to delegate. But even then - always question yourself if the task at hand really cannot be done by one of your most trusted people.

You will see that the more you delegate, the more time you have to focus on more strategic tasks. Your people will take over responsibility gladly in order to prove their potential. Remember added responsibility enriches their jobs.

Empowered employees who are not micromanaged are much more satisfied and productive. They are having more fun at work and are more creative than others.

Use delegation whenever possible. It will get you ahead, motivate your team, and help your most trusted people advance in their career as they become more visible in your organization.

Vision

"Where there is no vision, the people perish"

(Proverbs 29, 18 - King James Bible)

As a manager you have to have a clear vision of your life, your work and what you want to achieve. Anyone can follow a plan; most people can even be very efficient when following a plan! Only a leader has the vision that is transformed into the plan that others' can follow.

Being a visionary means being creative, thinking outside the box, trying to predict the future and knowing how you want to bend it. Don't be afraid of people telling you "You are too much of a visionary!"

Just because others can't see yet how to get to what you envision doesn't mean your vision is not feasible or wrong.

Being a visionary in your job means leaving all the rules and restrictions of the modern workplace behind, it means coming up with an idea of how to transform your business, your department and your work to reach something better.

Often this concept gets confused with mission statements or company strategies. However, those get so washed down they have lost all meaning. My favorite mission statement from one of the companies I have worked for was:

"We will provide the best possible service to our customer!"

Really? This is not a mission statement or a strategy, this is a given!

You and your company's vision are looking forward. It defines what your job or your company should look like in the future. You should be constantly defining this in all areas of your work. Challenge your team to work towards this vision as well. If you perform activities that do not support your vision, question yourself – are you doing something superfluous or is your vision not valid anymore? Don't hang on to yesterday's vision if it is not current anymore – be creative and come up with a better one.

Being a visionary will set you apart as a manager. You will be able to anticipate where your company is going and be in the prime position to move your team, your job and your company towards this vision.

Being a visionary will make you more important than your actual status in the company hierarchy – you will shape the success of your company!

That's it

„The whole is more than the sum of its parts."
Aristotle

Be efficient, be organized, be you, be a manager.
That doesn't sound too hard, does it?

Try it out!

I have tried to be very brief with you and give you some simple rules on how to manage and lead yourself, your team, department, organization or company. These rules work and I have proven them over the years with many different forms of teams.

These tips can be applied individually. Or, if you don't feel comfortable with one of them don't try it – be authentic in your way to manage. If it doesn't fit your management style, skip it and go on to the next rule. See if it works – be honest with yourself and give it a chance.

As I said in the beginning of this book – I did not invent these rules. They are a mixture of what I have learned through twenty years of work experience, studying for my MBA, and reading dozens of book on management or great business leaders.

(I highly recommend to start with "Who says Elephants can't dance" by Louis Gerstner and the Steve Jobs Biography by Walter Isaacson).

You will come up with your own set of rules and I encourage you to sit down and write down what works for you. Just the exercise of writing this book, has made these much clearer for myself and helped me personally to structure my work better and be more effective.

I would love to hear from you about your experience, feedback or your own rules and principles - you can contact me at joemeier@me.com and at my Blog http://risetothetop.net .

If you have enjoyed this book please leave some positive feedback on amazon.com - Thank you!

References

The 4-Hour Workweek, by Timothy Ferriss

Steve Jobs, by Walter Isaacson

Who says Elephants can't dance, by Louis Gerstner

Eat that Frog, by Brian Tracy

Our Iceberg is melting, by John P. Kotter

About the Author

Joe Meier has done consulting and held management positions in Information Technology for various Fortune 500 companies. He is currently an IT Director for a global consumer goods company.

Joe has studied Business Administration and holds a MBA from Heriott-Whatt University in Edinburgh, Scotland.

His first book "Rise to the top!" is a result of his twenty year career in an ever changing business environment. It is now available at Amazon.

You can reach Joe at joemeier@me.com or at his Blog http://risetothetop.net.